Between Gods

Between Gods

Poems by Donna Lewis Cowan

Cherry Grove Collections

Published by Cherry Grove Collections
P.O. Box 541106
Cincinnati, OH 45254-1106

ISBN: 9781936370672
LCCN: 2012933732

Poetry Editor: Kevin Walzer
Business Editor: Lori Jareo

Visit us on the web at website: www.cherry-grove.com

Acknowledgments

My thanks to the editors of the following publications: *Crab Orchard Review* ("Snow"), *DMQ Review* ("The Painter"), *32 Poems* ("Paris to Rome"), *Mannequin Envy* ("The Siren," "Children"), *Measure* ("Broken Sonnet: Eve Upon Awakening"), *Notre Dame Review* ("Klimt & Time," "Capture"), *The Worcester Review* ("Matisse's *Icarus Plate #8*," "Palette," "Home"), and *Fickle Muses* ("Virgo," "Daphne & Apollo: Meditations").

Thanks to my parents, Dorothy Mulligan and Donald Lewis, for encouraging me on this path with all their enthusiasm and love.

Thanks to my wonderful husband Jeff (o muse!) and my daughters, who refresh the world for me every day.

Special thanks go to Tom Gardner at Virginia Tech, without whose tutelage and encouragement this book could not have been written; and to Lucinda Roy, another extraordinary writer and professor in Blacksburg.

Finally, thanks to designer Terri Edillon, and editors Kevin Walzer and Lori Jareo, for making this project a work of art inside and out.

For my family on both coasts, and in-between

Table of Contents

1

2

3

4

1

Thaw

At the pond's edge the skaters steer
from the etched-out hollows, speed

toward the marrow mapped tight.
We are trying to outrace it, thaw

channeling into the grids - where you could
step through, surrender the balance

so tightly laced - your skate's slow blade
letting humours like a medieval cure,

the resistance like skin being tried
and its occasional accidental healing.

So you are an accomplice, shearing
the surface into further conquered

territories, into *what-will-happen*,
as where we stop the crystals shed

their science, drop their hierarchal
push and let go, spiked fibers beading

back into water, something our heat
cannot alter. We finish, our joined hands

dropping as magnets that have lost
their memory. How simple it is to leave

and be just a location, the new dew
spreading on our coats as you try

your hand at fire: our lit match
faith bent in the spreading wind.

Spring

1

Icicles loosen,
scattering like splintered spears
on the softened earth

2

More chores of spring's thaw:
a pond gathers new shoreline
into its borders

3

In aged grass, the stamp
fades where he had sanded her
into something else

4

New hands on his back
as the crescent moon steals light
from the sun, and runs

5

The moon spins from view,
blankets its craters and scars —
slips tides through their seams

Broken Sonnet: Eve Upon Awakening

You sleep, a shadow bent in careful candor
soft-grown among these chaoses of green,
and I awaken, my midnight visions mounting
the trees. Your fingers slip my hair; you wean
a decadence from my spring soul, counting
half-conscious strands that multiply and pour
hung ripeness on your cheek. What was that fruit
that picks from me the ripeness of this orchard?
Should I maintain these nights are merely duty?
O grief!…that tepid fingers are replaced
by tighter passions, your body's firm embrace
like a grounded planet. These lilies - upright, ruly -
cock their napes away like holy bells.
We shall make lithe blossoms remember themselves.

Children

In my basket they lay sober,
unlit: the unwinding scrolls
of newly-wired fuses.

I plant them in rows, grooming
the soil about the wooden embryos.

Surveyors of a broken sun,
they hum like untuned metal strings.

*

Spring, and their bodies snap
like sprung traps.

They hail revolution in the grass,
leaves lapping into dizzy,
strumming arms. Wide-eyed,
they swell hearts like wings.

*

It was a proud, metal winter,
stinging early March with stiff winds
and drunken rips of rain.

The farmers set out torches
to keep the groves from freezing.

We grazed our fingers
over your burrowing hoods,
pressing petals into their crowns,
warming you until the sun could.

*

Spring, and I watch you from my chair,
streaming electric, gathering gravity
around you like permanent planets.

I imagine the thread of your roots
wrapping this garden up tight –

each segment in the darkness
a maze of one world
finding another.

Wilderness

(Inspired by the creation myth of the Tlingit Indians in Southeast Alaska)

1. Water

You scattered sand from the sky, seeds
to grow islands. They rooted there
without light or reason, pushed shoots
into waters that scarcely moved,
holding the deep dreams of coins
which line a well, tossed and blessed.

Glaciers crawled, settled the spaces:
the waves turned blue silk, spindles
learning what they could yield.
They broke shore, steered it
back into the depths.
Water flashed through the fjords.

You rose from it, a totem.

2. Land

It is different with you, it requires
careful footing. Our footsteps track
fresh stitches in the sand.

Our edges are sharpened; we are careful.

We walk, feeling the distance
from that core,
a fire-magnet stirring.
When we stop
we are more than bodies
to grow feelings onto.

Our fingers touch,
a sanctum of skin.

We walk into the center of the world.

3. *Light*

She kept them in plain cedar boxes
(the sun, moon, and stars)
and light leaked from the lids
in blinding slices.

You longed to pin them finally to the skies,
and buried yourself in her skin,
grew in her flesh to capture them.

You threw the stars loose, and the moon,
and came back to me triumphant,
the sun in your pocket.

The track is a labyrinth of stars:
no turning back.

4. Man

A man is built from clay: simple.

But from this clay
life grows but cannot grow deep;
it is rough as sea-salt,
cannot hold.

A man's life is a gathering
of what falls, realignment.
I can feel it in your skin, volcanic,
what ripens, toughens, slides away.

How do I come after you,
settle you back into the mold,
compress,
release –

when I too am sifting off quietly
like crumbs carried away by ants.

5. Fire

The night begins its slow fuse
and we are inside the silence,
a kiln. The flames pull pigment
from the coals.

I fold you into icon,
circle you with fire:
a sly hieroglyph marking the holy.

The ashes writhe, shake off
a whisper of flame, grow brighter
as the wind gnashes them apart

in monument: a spearhead
honed and undiscovered.

Pitching Camp

You look up from what we have built

the quiet hewn like a star
a rugged brightness loosely mapped

Into this wood we hammer content

The quiet in you rears up whetted

Whatever roots we build
what we burrow into and make belong
are built from something else
or burned out from its essence

Whatever we bolt down
flares and vanishes

Taking the sinews apart
we see the green living root
that bends and holds

this night the stars invented

Daphne & Apollo: Meditations

1.

Beneath a hood of leaves, spiced
with new gold, I lean into bark -

Daphne in her escape,
not quite grown -

the jugular body of a woman silent
when Apollo turned his salty body against her,

his fingers
like flies against a windowpane.

She stood shuttered, let none
of the writhing slip

to the bark edges,
silenced the river winds,

that no breeze would sound
how her nimble body broke it,

how her pinions grooved the earth
and how she would rise, clean as jasper,

push to new heavens —
a fortress rising with sawed stones.

2.

She noticed first the looseness of the skin,
as if she had given birth,
but nothing, nothing:

never opened, emptied, sutured shut again,
never the raw, open-breathed fissure,
the breaking shoots of the garden.

She wondered, if she had arms to move,
could they round about a child,
would she warm its body with her own,

would it be more than taking Apollo -
the white-gold flash of him -
into them?...but the blooms about her

tightened, offered nothing;
their stems were stolid as crucifixes;
they touched only in strong winds.

3.

This was the time-edged terror of having it,
a vessel: the snap and snare
of her body opening, the sharp sweep
of recoiling leaves.

But Apollo could only love her;
he wisped his lyre strings with a sliver
of her silver bark, laurel woven
about its sea-wood throat.

The voice was new -
passion raised like the chronic sweat of flowers,
droplets like stones in a boy's tight fist
and dropped, scattering -

and it was not a chase: no lunging cries
or love notes pinned to tree-trunks,
kneeling and nipping a frail hand.
When he left her, she prayed

for a fatal discus to strike him,
that he might bloom beside her
and she would shade him
and his hollow conch-shell voice

which asked nothing.

Earth Prayer

I have slunk through mined streets,
trampled aching metal grates
bent like shut rainbows;

now I stir dream-paint,
search for the creeping rise of hills
where lie unborn flowers.

*

The sun weaves scarlet ribbons
through the clouds, strand by strand;
I milk the colors through my hands.

Ball-eyed fish gasp, grasp
from their pale mirror,
lunging at the potent air.

I am that rage at the still water's edge,
a shadow muffling the water lilies –

but remember he gave me flowers
wanting me always to feel life
spreading between my fingers.

*

I will be that flight
in which night meets bending day,

join the stars in full-bellied play,

and breathe the grasses' flavor through my cheek
(stroking the muscle beneath the startled dirt).

I will tremble as snowflakes gather at the sill,
clasping the glass with their chilling implosion;

pluck thick strings
and dance roundly in the darkness;

exalt in the mysteries of earth
where they deeply commune
in the silver hush of the moon.

2

The Painter

He divided her into eight equal parts
as any artist would, into architecture

and scale. Everything grew from the face,
descended into a pattern of pores.

He spent an hour in yellow, stirring
her eyelids into fire-consciousness.

He wanted to make her see something
outside the picture or beyond

his grey cracked window, hazardously
painted shut. He studied her, surfaced

the drowned anxieties of her skin,
the infant wrinkles. When she spoke

he could feel the image slip
from its solid monument

into division and when her voice
stopped he could assemble the pieces

again, the way a man would see her
without ever knowing her, as if beauty

was a need he could make.

The Siren

1.

And for each passing ship
the same song: a soulless
bare-breasted chorus line,
the blank verse braiding us in.

I lip-synch as you gather,
your hands tamping the ship rails
like hooves striking dust, catcalling,
applauding women who are children,
whose curiosity is never silent.

I would tell you: look at these rocks,
how the waves groom them
but leave the edges sharp,
how water trembles toward us
but shrinks away. Listen:
water peels a man's skin
like yellowed paper – you,
the quiet one, hear it and say nothing.

You are kindling for gods, dearest.

2.

I once sang. Once a man crawled close,
more blood than body, to tell me

I sounded like a cat in heat;
his palms snagged on the rocks
as he slid away. The boat's cabin
shuddered like an egg sac in a storm.

I felt my voice empty into the salty air,
blend into the sea like rain –
diminuendo…then nothing.

The sea drew close,
lapped out its silences,
divinities,
bones.

3.

Already the sea
is trying to forget: it recedes
like a potion used, corked,
and put away again.

Without love, life flows from you
like guttered rain. Why else
would these rocks lie blanketed
by so many outstretched hands?

Is it only your map –
that innocent geometry
of stars –
that will not fail you?

Moonblind

Last night we left time unopened.

But how suddenly this place
crafts itself into sun, forest, air.
Night dovetails into the hollows
and is gone.

The sun slowly brick-lays
circumference.
How else would we find our way back
to what we are?–
when we would be simply
skin and seed, or wind tangling
these leaves.

And time pools before us
like so much spillage.

Fallen

The air is wide and graphic.
We bend at the edge
of this cliff's table,

stacking chips
without counting them, throwing
the final wager of this night.

The waves blend, wheel —
spider-web
spindling strands,

caulking the branches
of loose-fingered trees
of coral. You jump narrowly

into that terrible forest -
the veils of surf
between the rocks -

wind umbilical through
a steel-glass sheet of sky,
skin shot silver.

The planets are drumming
discourse. After far too long
you emerge, eyes matching mine,

telegraphic, buzzing fire:
the current
shocks the source.

Paris to Rome

We arrived after the Iraq invasion,
before the European heat wave
and during the usual transit strike
as if we could dash between

the tomes of history, just to see
the sights. We're doubled up
in the cars, too many of us
awake in the sleeper.

We go deeper into countryside
and the houses recede further
from the tracks, as if
this is not what was wanted,

or not entirely – the tourists learning
towns from their transit maps
but still mispronouncing them,
rendering *Saint Cloud*

a Yankee god of precipitation.
What was it for?– these meadows
cleared of their nostalgic flowering
where the tracks cut through.

We are sealed from sound
but the rhythms steep in our skin.
Call it antidote: the track divined
and steady over rough terrain.

At Pinecrest Lake

It's not the heat, it's the humidity,
you said, as if it were a bad choice,

a fixture that could be rewired,
set to modern code. The air staggers,

heavy with its stale lint:
the cast-offs of pillow-white clouds

far above this grainy untidiness.
The world makes fewer demands

than in freshly-peeled spring,
when grass, now at half-mast,

leapt up as if clearing hurdles.
It understands how we are immersed,

the air saturated, our bodies in futile
dog-paddle, scooped up like minute

life clinging to sand in her shovel -
who make the best of it

with the innocence of sandcastles -
trying to survive the lifting-away,

a randomness like cards shuffling,
here a pair of hearts, or not,

draw another card. I reach for you,
start the process though our processes

overlap at only one point,
knowing we are only a cross-section

of this: the sky's dissolving layers,
the earth being broken again

into her plastic bucket,
the brave bacteria

now separated from their colony
that harvest wherever they land.

Penelope

Now four years of fraying wool
on the loom - my hands grey,
splintered as never before -
and once the tapestry is finished,
anything may happen. We are so
vulnerable to magic; one may be raped
by swans; none of it is hearsay.

I have heard you are lover to a woman
who could keep you with her forever –
and what a trick!

Here the soldiers' wives use each other
for company; the handmaids touch
my skin as they touch my gowns,
with windy light fingers, out of habit –
pressing harder only to coax
the wrinkles out. One stray touch
and my skin is alive for hours –

that is loneliness, a pair of hands
winding through that medusa
of strands, soothing the loose ends
into patience, into new fabric
to blanket a man's body:

Laertes', yours,
a stricken soldier's, or perhaps
the body of that drunk exposed suitor

from the courtyard, having tripped
over his mind once too often.
He tells me his semen is wine
drawn from the rarest of sea-violets,

and reports gossip from the docks
of your sinuous beach-wrests
with angry goddesses. A vast,
voiceless sea, but the gods have ears
and yes, eyes – eyes growing like moons
as you drive glory slowly,
absently, into the sand.

Klimt and Time: Three Poems

1. *Nouveau*

Then it was hinged in:
a parlor-scene's exact history,

its gold-plated frame
greater than the picture,

casting vines that circle and ravel
with the stamp of primitive eyes.

They tangle about her
as she stares out, her soul

a drowsy prattle at the pane.
She is stunned still,

a jarred specimen watching
as the forest rises about her,

as visitors pause, then accelerate
toward the masterpiece in the next gallery:

tanned Judith in her golden collar,
the woman who had her way.

2. Sunflower

Square off the horizon,
razor the sky, and let the poppies

fend for themselves. It is a body
they hoist, a sunflower overgrown

by its leaves in a cloak
of hooked spades, given up

to the sharpening petals below.
It seeks the sun long edited out,

mixed with the cutting-room scraps,
the square canvas pruning the spread

of petal and sky. Its head snaps
into paralysis, mounted there,

the unlocked florets softening for descent,
less a proud crown than a creature

tousling in a trap,
whose life you cannot give back.

3. Portrait of Emilie Flöge

You fill me in, set my face into
a measured hollow like a jewel;

the fabric evolves from the rocks:
a netting of sea-strands, loose cells.

You shadow length and width,
from a distance or up close, inside,

between, against, pushing
the parameters open as a study,

creating new versions of skin,
each body *a priori* knowledge,

at least when you begin.
You know I won't stay here,

that dimensions have stops
(that we are always documenting,

like *this*) though they continue forever.
And here is the marker:

my hand moves through the beam,
emerging intact on the other side

like a magic trick. You dare me
to want what I want:

for all symmetry to break off
and banish its twin.

3

Capture

(After Rilke's "Der Panther")

You waited this long, through all
the translations. *Heart* and *bars*
are the simplest of nouns - recoverable -
but too many words describe

what you missed: *sphere, light,*
world, life. The bars are gone,
now engineered glass fencing
a jungle of approximations.

Something to get used to,
that mirror. When you look further
you see us walking our own
concrete hills, now equally

distorted by reflection. In 1902
when you stood knotted
in ornamental iron, at least
we would have breathed the same air;

I would hear the dried grass
shattering as you paced
the perimeter, spacing time
like a snare-drum's cracks.

(Noun:
a member of a class of words

distinguished by its plural
and possessive endings.)

If I see tenderness in your eyes
it can't be documented; it would be
fitting force through a needle's eye
into the neat fiber of quatrain.

Hu-po

(Hu-po in Chinese means "tiger's soul" – it was once believed that at death, the soul sank underground and was transformed into amber.)

1. Transformation

The tiger finds its paws among bones,
awakens to its slowing blood,
its black nest. The soul
drifts from the body,
molten fire.

Turning the soil,
they find the gold resin
emptied there like minor water
from high falls.

2. Amulet

He prowls, appraises me
from behind an amulet's walls -
filled with the trapped breath
of a thousand years, sealed
like a season absorbing
a season - kilned and honed
by various sun-striped skies.

It is the size of an eye
but is carved into a heart.

Is this what was longed for,
the seismic, hot hive of surrender?

Home

1.

It is there as you cross the hall,
the floor's slope pulled back

two degrees, adrenalin as your body
catches the drop with high-wire balance.

The floorboards escape from their grain,
sprout new designs: puddled ringlets, pearls;

or here, an evolution of the earthworm,
a diagram for study of the segments,

a looking-up after each move
like old pinups, the pose inched open

with each page flip.

2.

In 1942 these hills were numbered
and chain-linked; the earth shuffled.

It was something small, as if the world
could be reduced to house-hunting,

polite footsteps and peering around corners,
turning the knobs – something other than

the slow-motion then zoom lens
of the telegram. Say it was a woman,

stepping out of her life
that was meanwhile – pacing

the flat geography of pain. Was it enough
to be encased in brick, to know

the dirt uprooted and tamped back down
would re-inhabit its original strength, someday?

3.

The craters in the plaster, the brushstrokes,
suggest they built with old tools

that slandered the wanted precisions
of their minds and hands.

And so our rooms sink and expand,
their variables longing to return

to their original values: the brick shears off
from the clustered chimney, the rootless wood

tightens and compresses; the steel beams
are less certain they want to support this enterprise.

With each footstep we help this wood
give itself away.

The Door

1. Pigment

I am painting it again,
making the room smaller
with each layer,
as if painting myself
into a corner -

until the grain is dissolved
by brushstroke.

2. Entrances

Glass door knobs seem frivolous
on these solid oak doors.

They fascinate her; when you are three
each door knob is a glass carnation,
blooming in its brass spindle
with the keyhole beneath,
mushroom-shaped and long empty.

(A carnation for its optimism,
its rigid symmetry - a hardiness
appropriate for button-holes
at weddings, standing up
to the pin through its stem.)

Glass, for metal was needed
for tanks' skin, but as useless
as any skin proves to be
(like all borders, making
the target visible,
what you aim for).

3. Keyhole

Her eye's hazel shine
swings into the keyhole;
in a moment she will realize
all that is not in the room
with her.

Then the shuffle of her feet
in retreat, moving to the next door
for the next game.

I am here, now.

Now I am gone.

4. Locksmith

He readies the house
for a soldier coming home,
saved by the right wound.

He fits the metal plate
into the oak grooves,

screws it into place.

The key gleams.

Now it is up to you
to create the hidden.

Navigation

Our tent rests at the cusp
of skyline. Beyond our mesh door

petals sift the air, weightless charms
that might dangle a child's wrist.

When the wind pulls us from the static,
we steel against the covered earth

but are steered into landscape
along with our resistance, with leaves

walled into the hollow logs, each pounded
into the shape of a navigable life.

Virgo

She bundles in speechless layers of white,
each curve an afterthought. Her hem
bobbing at her ankles, she holds a shaft of wheat,
an ear of corn, between thin-boned fingers.

She will not raise eyelids, skirts, issues.

Her last cry may be from the belly of a volcano.
She pleases gods.

Her mind wears a scarlet alphabet,
spells out all the names and midnight harvests
her body closes with a ring.

She may marry late.
She may never marry.

The lion always comes before her.

Night upon night,
that stiff position
is pinned in the stars.

Returning to Blacksburg

1.

Still here, the limestone buildings
and their corresponding trees
crowd into the spotlights,
darkness measured and tossed between.

Shading the stone arc is an evergreen,
its wily electric green
bending like a willow
while the stern green-mud pines

remain stiff. The leaves rupture
into armored feathers, pairing on branches
in varied doses, collaborating
on perimeter, tapering into hesitant arcs.

At the border they are dog-eared,
their needles stumped like broken spokes,
where the shift from vacant air
into vascular fiber must be softened.

The rest fold in a banner against
the trunk, saving themselves,
as last-born flax lilies await
vibration into bloom.

2.

Wind swerves through the trees,
dividing the absorbed, the detoured,
the crashed atoms. The leaves tip up,
then dip, symmetry balancing

what is likely to survive. A swan
divides the water into coiled channels,
sending the synapses back
to be caught downstream.

3.

Time is still in play, reversing its revisions:
the trick of the evergreen gathering
its tactics. Moss patterns on these stones,

borrows water to leave its stain -
a counterfoil - the way that what I give you
and what I keep are the same.

4

Transplant

It is what you wanted: to be emptied
and filled. Still it surprised you how

easily you came undone, how simply light
laid down where your mind so long

forwarded its furies, the stilled heart
that planned ahead, rationed, failed.

Now it is ahead of you, the trigger
of a need you didn't plan for, titanium-lit

in the dark skeleton, crystallized by voltage.
You imagine it keeping you within bounds

like cruise control, binding the inevitable
heart-race in its endless loop -

or is its job to keep up, not decide? -
making your life linear, as if your desires

were riding the scales programmed
in code, to be bucked off at any time.

You think you were saved for a reason,
even found Ararat on a map

so the degrees of latitude and longitude
could help you believe. That is not our world,

we would be the ones left behind.
With its fish-bone creases your scar

resembles a fossil: the evidence that closes
the case, but which further evidence can erase.

Axes

The sun incubates
in a pale corner of sky.

The weather vane flips,
scalps the loose air, strains

steel in divine offering.
It spins a rusted warning,

a tribal dance winding
its tangled flames, mowing dirt

into blackness. The crowning
shadow of the steel rooster

splits, grows along the building
back; taut-feathered wind

shuts the vane into its axis,
into precision: a trapped

phonograph record,
78 r.p.m. I shiver,

wait for the diamond needle
to be lifted.

Calypso

Metal waves gather the island,
their grey shocks dragging sand
into an empty womb. Her footsteps
break shore like tissue. She shaves
the edges away, follows the ship's
vined shadow. His image chills her
like stone sharpening the spine
of the sea. He does not see her there,

her skirts floating the water
like a hyacinth. *Dawn is the birth
of shadow*, she thinks,
drawing men back to the sea
as surely as sirens' lips
would skirt them back to shore –

as surely as she had loved him,
raising her body to him like a limb.

She knows the limits of any vessel;
a woman is never a closed thing:
torn from the inside-out
and reassembled, all fire before
the quiet tucking-under of wings.

Snow

Flakes scramble from the mist - white
streaming like a new constellation -
and as quickly their paths end,

found and defined by their collision.
It is something to be measurable,
to add up – each click into place

a vanishing into ritual, flakes
unlacing into thaw, night grinding
this faceted rind smooth

to support our weight, or not.
We walk the undisturbed angles
that drift missed, the sudden

blacktop where snow has forked
like defectors' footsteps. We are slow
through this foreign gravity,

even our voices softened
by interference, its white noise.
It is tenderness, this overflow –

there was room for more all along.
And we had tired of edges,
the elms blank in compatible rows

where now they merge, their iced
buckling like monuments steadied
in marble, taking up space

they had given up. What does it say
of us that we needed this so badly,
all this - the blanketed bicycle still

bare between its spokes, the shovel
waiting, both metal mechanisms
of speed - now one world,

a seating chart we would otherwise resist,
as if we would know where we belong
if given the chance.

Matisse's *Icarus Plate #8*

1.

If He had wanted any man
to be so bold, such a point-blank
essence, He would have raised him

on the first day, while weaning light
from darkness – the violent extraction
as if shearing nerves from skin

never touched. He is all shadow,
so we must imagine his foundation:
the slender hollow of his belly

as if a spine had been pulled from it,
as if the bold strokes of his body
stood for themselves.

2.

As the stars claw into minds of fir,
we ask if, here, Icarus falls or flies,

if he has broken that middle ground,
grappled at its roots, turned the thin soil

until there was nothing left to conquer,
just the sun above, a held vial waiting to spill.

Perhaps he has been there and falls from it,
his arms caught in wings' weight and the tempest

of flight, his body rough in that mirror-cold
square of sky, and only his heart a careful red circle.

Thingvellir, Iceland

A few white houses, a lone church,
are propped up here, the window boxes

plumed with primary colors
as if arrival could happen at any time.

A black mountain balances the night sky
just as the sea pinged back blue

into daylight; there is no need for apology.
Some grass is allowed through; the green patches

among its retractions like stepping stones.
At the highest point the wind is unharnessed,

seals us into place. They tell us
the plates separate two centimeters per year.

Rock turns liquid on unbounded time scales,
spins land apart like mirrored conveyor belts,

tucks the excess beneath the sea,
creating a new place.

Is it an absence?
Or a line against which to choose sides,

remain on separate playing fields
as the rock crawls silently beneath us,

defying its printed geography,
aligning us into the ranks

of those who know better,
would never build their houses there;

though the earth refuses to expand,
consumes itself at the same speed

that it grows, so we can't see
from this distance

what will never be the same.

Cleaning *Lincoln Logs*

The impossible task:
making our leftovers
clean enough for a daughter.

In my hands the dust
patterns like animal tracks,
crosses the abbreviated grooves
worn away by over-love,

the stress of building
and knocking down the structure
too easily, too often.

You empty the scratches
where you etched
letters, initials,

before you knew
how the world
could whittle away
each masterpiece.

Drying in the sun,
they are still alive —

the rings of a hundred years
are captured, translated
into new time. Later

in the red imaginations
of our bodies we build
and burn the cabins;

we burn them
from the inside out.

Palette

She has taken over the picture
with a toddler's thick black lines,
striking through my plotted leaves -

this is what matters - dissecting
the pointillist penciling
best viewed from a distance.

The strike-through precision
of her crayon almost Modernist,
as Picasso would secure a frame

for each primary color, a roping-off
from what surrounds it.
Spelling it out: *This will help you,*

with your aging eyes — too old
to have a daughter this young,
too hesitant to finish this tree

on paper: have I started in the right
place, how deep have these roots
grown and do I keep them

invisible as an iceberg's core,
the ballast that battens down
the shine? The trick is

to sketch the borders
before it moves, because it will.
Now I can see the branches

loaded like springs;
I can see time unwinding
my steady hand.

About the Author

Donna Lewis Cowan's poetry has appeared in numerous journals including *Crab Orchard Review, DMQ Review, Notre Dame Review, Measure: A Review of Formal Poetry,* and *The Worcester Review.* A technical writer and programmer as well as poet, she lives in the Washington, D.C. suburbs with her family. Her blog is www.donnalewiscowan.wordpress.com.

CPSIA information can be obtained at www.ICGtesting.com
Printed in the USA
LVOW091742280312

275129LV00001B/9/P